ART APPRECIATION
FOR THE
POPSICLE GENERATION

Written and illustrated by
Lauann Brown

*A Handbook of Ideas
to Teach Art Appreciation
in the Elementary School*

Cover by Vanessa Filkins

Copyright © Good Apple, Inc., 1984

ISBN No. 0-86653-172-6

Printing No. 987654321

GOOD APPLE, INC.
BOX 299
CARTHAGE, ILLINOIS 62321-0299

TABLE OF CONTENTS

IS IT WORTH IT?

If you're thinking about spending some time talking to children about art, good for you! We've all heard people say, "I don't know a thing about art, but I know what I like." I always chuckle when I hear that. It reminds me of a toddler at the table who refuses to try a new dish because he knows what he likes. What joys we miss when we close our minds to new ideas! Just as the toddler's mother entices her child with a spoonful of the new dish, we can encourage our students to know art. We can educate them by introducing them to the world of art and teaching them the priceless value of our artistic heritage. We, who are fortunate enough to share these experiences with young children, gain new insights from the curious and unique perspective which looking and talking about art with the young provides. Fortunately, you don't have to be an expert art critic, or historian, to accomplish this goal. I've put together a few easy-to-do suggestions in this book to help you make it fun. After all, learning about art should be as refreshing as a Popsicle on a hot summer's day! TRY IT!

CHAPTER 1

TIPS
FOR TEACHERS

GUARANTEED BOREDOM

This formula guarantees surefire boredom:

* Use vocabulary words that your students are not familiar with to explain works of art.

* Choose prints they cannot relate to.

* Always lecture and cut short discussion times.

* Act bored.

* Use an excessive amount of time.

* Follow the same format lesson after lesson.

* Act as if art is something to be put on a pedestal, totally unrelated to the students' everyday experiences.

DO YOUR HOMEWORK

Before you present a lesson, read as much as you can about your subject. Excellent materials are available in children's sections of most libraries. Don't overlook familiar children's magazines which often feature articles about art, works of art, or artists. Many new audiovisual sources are available for teacher use through private companies, museums, and local school districts. Start picture files on individual artists, subjects, or media. Collect prints to use in games and class discussions. Keep your eyes open...sources for inspiration are everywhere!

YOUR ATTITUDE IS THE FIRST IMPRESSION A CHILD WILL RECEIVE ABOUT THE WORLD OF ART.

KID'S CHOICE

Research has indicated that children prefer:
BRIGHT COLORS
REALISM
FAMILIAR SUBJECT MATTER

When making selections to discuss in the elementary school, keep these points in mind, but do **not** limit your selections to those works that have only these characteristics. Also consider:

* Examples that most clearly illustrate your objective.
* Large, clear examples that the class can view easily.
* Examples that you feel positive about (your bias always shows).
* Several examples are usually better than just one. (Three Van Goghs illustrate his short brushstrokes better than one example. Comparison between work that does illustrate the concept and work that does not will make the ideas clearer to the students.)

SHOW AND TELL

*   Children are eager to share their discoveries about art. Allow a special time in class for "Art Show and Tell."

*   Put up an Art News bulletin board to display news articles, cartoons, or other art-related articles from local newspapers.

*   Set up an Art Corner for display of objects the children bring to school.

*   Take time to discuss and share their feelings.

DECK THE WALLS

Take over your favorite empty wall by featuring displays. Ask for prime space in the cafeteria, library, or office area of your school. Choose a spot where students gather. Take tips from Madison Avenue...ADVERTISE! Use catchy slogans, ask leading questions, poke fun, and spark imaginations. Make art fun!

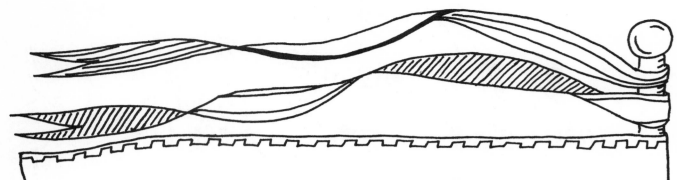

THE REAL THING

As good as the finest slides, films, or reproductions can be, THERE'S NOTHING LIKE THE REAL THING! Seeing an authentic painting, drawing, or sculpture reveals more than any photo or copy of it can ever hope to do. Whenever possible, show the class an original work of art. How?

...GET OUT OF CLASS!

Take advantage of local art-related sources. Visit an artist's studio, a nearby gallery, an art show in the park, a local craftsman's shop, or the nearest university art department. Take walking tours to discover local architecture, community monuments, graphic designs on billboards, or backyard folk art. Look at nature and compare artists' interpretations of similar landscapes. Watch the changes in weather, the seasons, and shadows. Take a look at your school from the outside.

GUEST APPEARANCES

Invite guests from your community to school. Parents, grandparents, local artists, travelers, representatives from a craft group, and theater companies are often eager and willing to come to school to share their knowledge or demonstrate their skills.

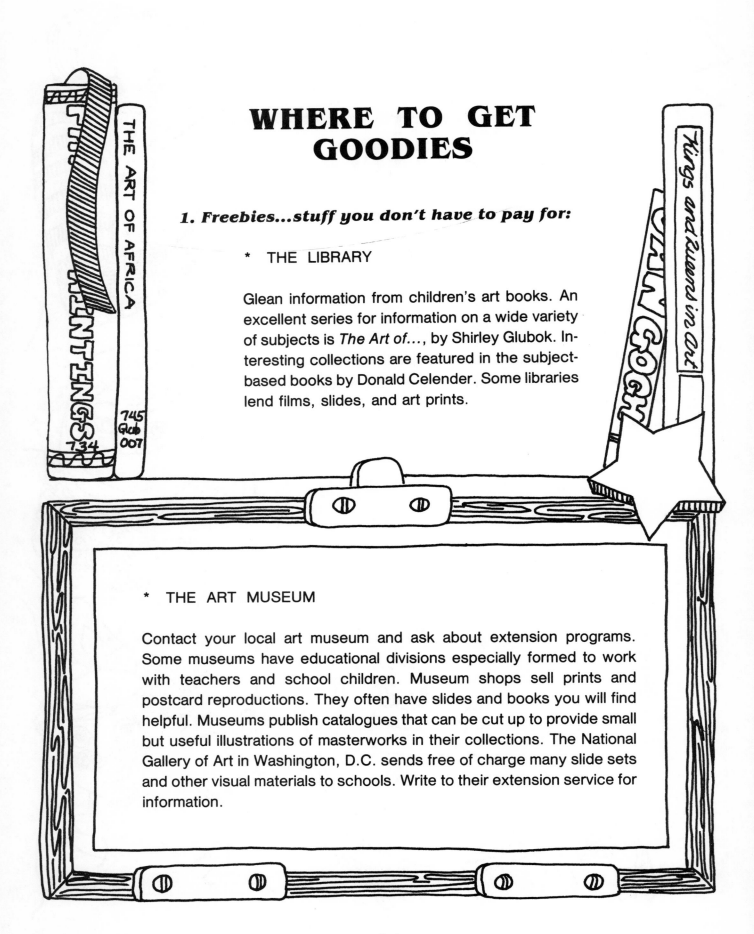

WHERE TO GET GOODIES

1. Freebies...stuff you don't have to pay for:

* THE LIBRARY

Glean information from children's art books. An excellent series for information on a wide variety of subjects is *The Art of...*, by Shirley Glubok. Interesting collections are featured in the subject-based books by Donald Celender. Some libraries lend films, slides, and art prints.

* THE ART MUSEUM

Contact your local art museum and ask about extension programs. Some museums have educational divisions especially formed to work with teachers and school children. Museum shops sell prints and postcard reproductions. They often have slides and books you will find helpful. Museums publish catalogues that can be cut up to provide small but useful illustrations of masterworks in their collections. The National Gallery of Art in Washington, D.C. sends free of charge many slide sets and other visual materials to schools. Write to their extension service for information.

2. *Pay 4's...stuff that costs money:*

* THE POST OFFICE

The post office sells a Masterworks Commemorative Stamp Kit. They make nice tiny reproductions for art games. If you ask, the postmaster may save outdated posters from the post office promotions for you. (They occasionally feature artists, a work of art, or a process you will talk about in class.)

* MAGAZINES

Art magazines have nice reproductions. You can build a collection of prints from *School Arts, Arts and Activities,* and covers of *Instructor* magazines. Some children's magazines have articles about art and artists. Start a tear sheet file of art reproductions, individual artists, and processes used in making art.

* MAKE YOUR OWN

If you are handy with a camera, start snapping slides of local architecture, works of art in your community, or craftsmen at work.

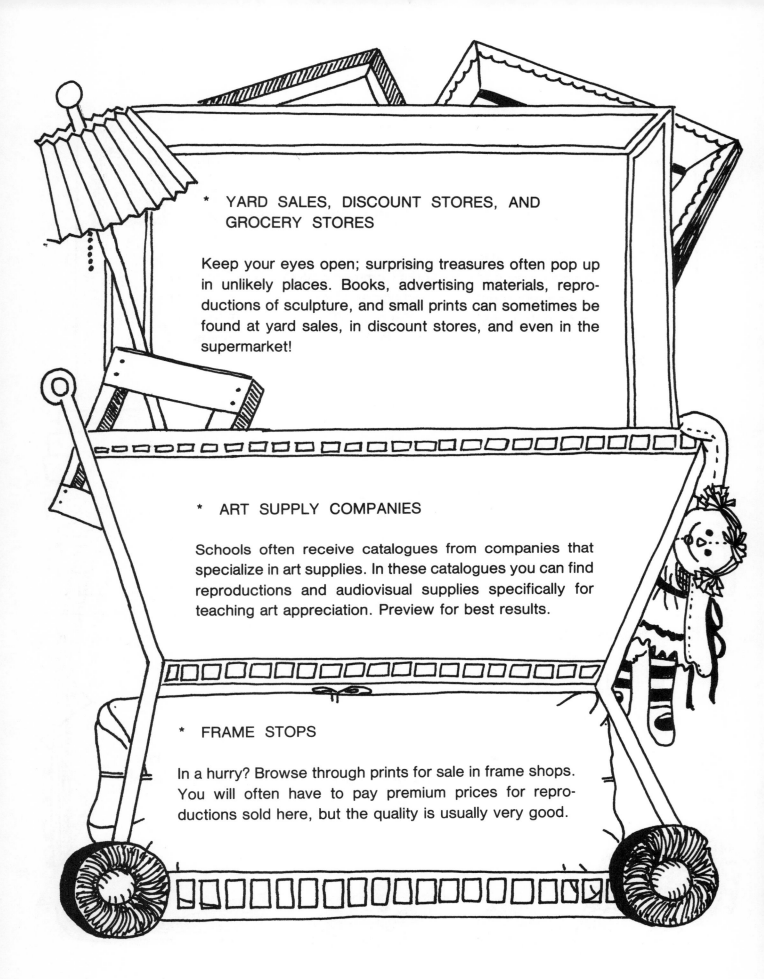

* YARD SALES, DISCOUNT STORES, AND
  GROCERY STORES

Keep your eyes open; surprising treasures often pop up
in unlikely places. Books, advertising materials, reproductions of sculpture, and small prints can sometimes be
found at yard sales, in discount stores, and even in the
supermarket!

* ART SUPPLY COMPANIES

Schools often receive catalogues from companies that
specialize in art supplies. In these catalogues you can find
reproductions and audiovisual supplies specifically for
teaching art appreciation. Preview for best results.

* FRAME STOPS

In a hurry? Browse through prints for sale in frame shops.
You will often have to pay premium prices for reproductions sold here, but the quality is usually very good.

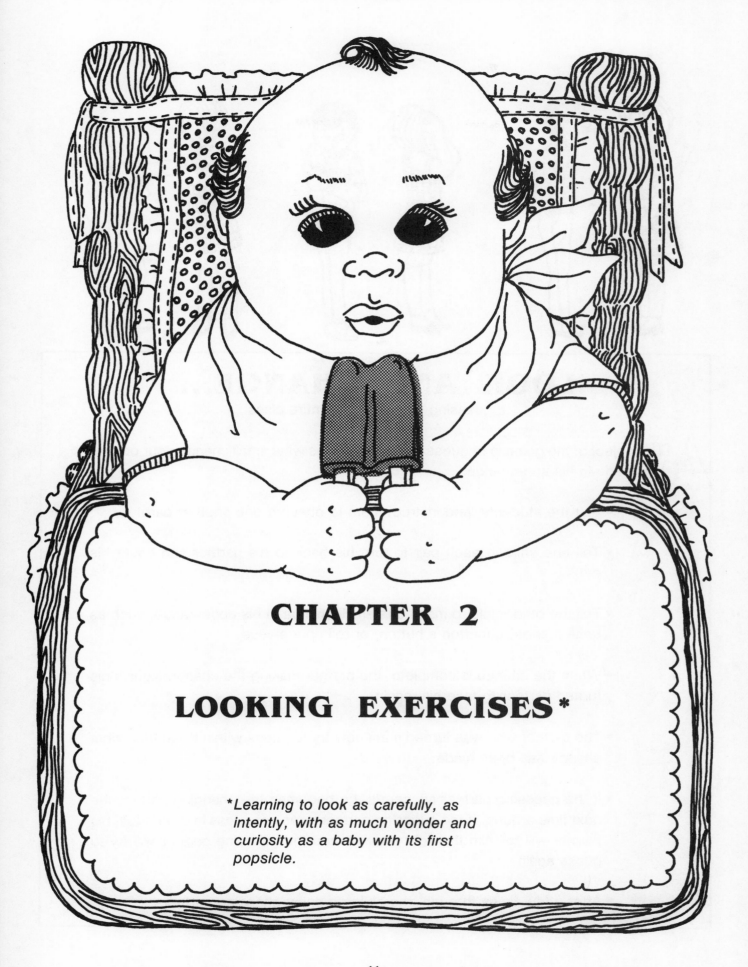

CHAPTER 2

LOOKING EXERCISES*

*Learning to look as carefully, as intently, with as much wonder and curiosity as a baby with its first popsicle.

LOOK AND CHANGE...
a guessing game for the entire class

The object of the game is to guess within three tries what small change your partner has made in his appearance.

- Pair the students, and instruct them to observe one another carefully.

- Tell one child in each pair to turn his back to his partner and cover his eyes.

- Tell the other child to make one small change in his appearance, such as untie a shoe, unbutton a button, or roll up a sleeve.

- When the change is complete, the partner making the change signals his turned partner to face him again.

- The partner who was turned must now try to guess within three tries what change has been made.

- If the guessing partner succeeds, he becomes the changing partner the next time around. If the guessing partner does not guess in three tries, his partner will tell him the right answer, and the guessing partner will try to guess again.

- After a few times through, the children enjoy changing partners.

MIRRORS...

a game of concentration and observation for the entire class

The object of the game is to perform in unison so well that an observer would not be able to tell who is the person and who is the mirror.

- Pair the students and let them choose one person in each pair to be "it." The second person will be the mirror and will try to copy the movements of the person who is "it." The students cannot talk, or touch, during the action. They must communicate with each other by moving slowly and maintaining eye contact.

- Demonstrate with a partner.

- Let the children practice. Circulate and observe. Offer suggestions when needed.

- After a time, instruct the partners to reverse roles.

- Discuss the experience. Ask:
  — Was it easier to be "it" or the mirror.
  — What kinds of movements were difficult, what kinds were easy?
  — How did you feel when you and your partner worked well together?

- Repeat the exercise. Let pairs who want to demonstrate to the class.

- Let the class try to decide who is "it."

13

LEMONS...

an activity for the entire class observing unique characteristics

The object of the exercise is to recognize your lemon.

- Pass around a box of lemons. Have each child choose one.

- Tell each child to look carefully at his/her lemon, taking note of each small and unique characteristic that makes the lemon special.

- Have each child name his/her lemon, introduce it to the class, and tell what it is about the lemon that is special.

- Put all the lemons back into the box.

- Have the children come to the box a few at a time and find their lemons.

- Repeat the exercise using the sense of touch.
  - Each child examines his lemon by feeling, not looking.
  - Put the lemons back into the box, six at a time, and have the children find their lemons blindfolded.

3" X 5" CARD TRICKS...

two learning center activities for individuals

Color Swatches

- Glue paint sample swatches (from paint stores) on individual 3" x 5" cards.

- Have the children arrange them:
    — From lightest to darkest
    — From one color to another (red to yellow)
    — From brightest to dullest
    — From warmest to coolest

Lines

- Draw a variety of lines with various media on the cards.

- Have the children sort them into categories, such as
    — Thick or thin
    — Curved or straight
    — Vertical, horizontal, or diagonal

BUTTONS INTO BABY FOOD JARS...

a learning center activity

- Have the child match and sort buttons into baby food jars by:
    - — Color
    - — Size
    - — Shape
    - — What they are made of
    - — Texture
    - — Number of Holes
    - — Type of Shank
    - — Etc.

SEQUENCING MOVING OBJECTS...

a learning center activity

- Collect a series of illustrations from cartoon strips, comic books, or magazines that show a sequence of movement, such as a car goes off into the distance, Superman flies closer, a train whizzes past, etc.

- Mount the sections on separate pieces of tagboard.

- Put matching sections in an envelope.

- Give each child an envelope and have him arrange the sections in order.

GUESS MY EXPRESSION...

a classroom activity

- Make one or more 10" x 15" cardboards with a horizontal rectangle cut about 3" from the 10" end.

- Use the cardboards to demonstrate expressions, masking off all but your eyes, or mouth.

- Have the children guess your expressions, or demonstrate expressions using the cardboards themselves.

- Discuss:
    — What happens to your eyes when you are (happy, sad, mad, or scared)?
    — What happens to your mouth when you are (happy, sad, mad, or frightened)?

- Look at prints and discuss facial expressions in each one.

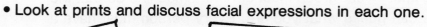

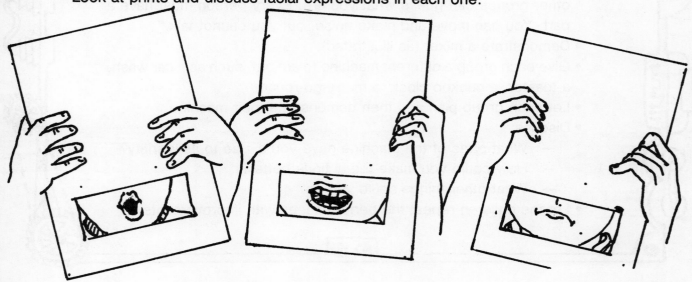

CARTOON FACE
EXPRESSIONS...

a learning center activity matching words with expressions

• Collect a series of faces from newspaper comic strips, coloring books, or magazines that show strong emotion, such as fear, anger, sorrow, joy and surprise.

• Mount the faces on the same size tagboard cards.

• Make a series of word cards that state a feeling, such as fear, anger, sorrow, surprise or joy.

• Have the children match the faces with the words.

• LATER, YOU MIGHT SUBSTITUTE FACES FROM PRINTS THAT SHOW EMOTION.

Related Studio Activity: Have the children draw their own faces several times on the same piece of paper, changing their expressions each time. A mirror is useful for this activity.

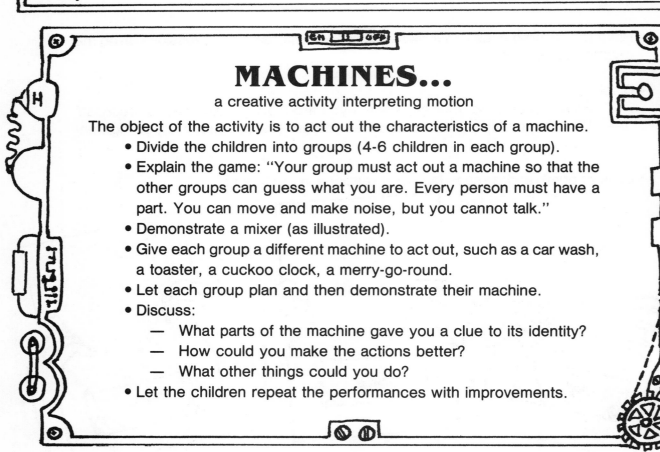

MACHINES...

a creative activity interpreting motion

The object of the activity is to act out the characteristics of a machine.

• Divide the children into groups (4-6 children in each group).

• Explain the game: "Your group must act out a machine so that the other groups can guess what you are. Every person must have a part. You can move and make noise, but you cannot talk."

• Demonstrate a mixer (as illustrated).

• Give each group a different machine to act out, such as a car wash, a toaster, a cuckoo clock, a merry-go-round.

• Let each group plan and then demonstrate their machine.

• Discuss:
  — What parts of the machine gave you a clue to its identity?
  — How could you make the actions better?
  — What other things could you do?

• Let the children repeat the performances with improvements.

CHECKLIST...

a listing activity for learning centers or classroom

- Choose a print. Prepare a list of as many things as possible that you see in it. (They can be objects, shapes, lines, colors, patterns, or textures.)

- Have the children look at the print and try to memorize what they see.

- Hide the print from their view.

- Pass out copies of the checklist or read it aloud. Have the students indicate what things they remember from the checklist, what things they overlooked.

- Show the print again and find the items on the checklist.

WHICH PIECE BELONGS?...
a learning center activity

- Select a print that you have several copies of. Cut a square from one print. Set this square and the print aside.

- Cut squares from the other prints in the same general vicinity as you did from the first print. Vary the placement slightly. Save the squares from these prints but discard the prints themselves.

- Mount the first print and all the squares on a piece of poster board. Label the squares "A," "B," "C," etc. Letter "Which Piece Belongs?" on the top of the poster board.

- Have the child decide, by looking, which square came from the first print. (Provide an answer key on the back of the poster.)

MATCHING PARTS...
a learning center activity

• Collect a series of magazine photographs, illustrations, or art reproductions that picture a single object. Mount them on tagboard.

• Cut each of these into four pieces.

• Put all the pieces in a stack and mix up the piles.

• Have the children find which parts belong together. (You can key the backs with numbers for a self-check device.)

(Some children will enjoy playing a card game with these parts. Dealing the parts, drawing from each other, and making sets are the elements of a simple version. The child with the greatest number of matching sets at the end of play wins. Older children enjoy the game with architecture cards.)

 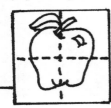 

POINT OF VIEW...
a sorting activity for the learning center

• Collect a series of magazine pictures or art prints that illustrate a specific point of view (as seen from above, below, beside, behind, in front of).
• Mount them. Have the children sort them into these categories:
   — I am above the scene looking down.
   — I am below the scene looking up.
   — I am in front of the scene looking in.
   — I am behind the scene looking out.
• Follow-Up: Look at prints, as a class, and discuss specific points of view. Talk about how you can tell what point of view an artist has used.

WHO, OR WHAT, AM I?...

a classroom activity

• Select a print that has many small details, or a variety of shapes.

• Choose one object, or shape, from the print and fill in this list on a 3" x 5" card:

I am above _____.

I am below _____.

I am to the right of _____.

I am to the left of _____.

Who, or what, am I?

• Make one for each student describing a different object or shape.

• Give each child a card, and let him/her try to solve the riddle.

• A variation is to let the children make up the riddle cards.

FORGERY...
a classroom exercise in remembering visual characteristics

- Choose a print that you have several copies of. Leave one of the prints unaltered, but change each of the remaining prints in a minor way, such as thicken a line, add a pattern to a solid area, change the color in a particular section.

- Show the class the original unaltered print. Give them time to study it carefully with their eyes.

- Take away the original print. Show the class an altered copy.

- Ask them if this is an original form or a forgery. See if they can identify the change.

- Repeat the questioning with the other altered copies of the print. (Slip the original into the sequence to jar students' memories.)

- At the end of the questioning, line all the prints up and have the children reidentify which are the forgeries, and which is the unaltered print.

DETECTIVE...

a learning center game for one or more

The object of the game is to match pieces from prints to the originals.

- Cut small pieces from prints that you have duplicates of.

- Give the child the small pieces and the unaltered copies of the prints.

- See if the child can match the pieces to the prints. (Key the pieces to the prints on the back for self-checking.)

I found it!

25

SHAPE FIND...
an active search game for the entire class

The object of the game is to find the source of the greatest number of shapes in a given time period.

- Choose a series of prints that have a variety of interesting shapes.

- Label each of these prints with a letter of the alphabet by clipping a 3" x 5" card with a letter on it to the print.

- Cut at least one 5" x 5" piece of acetate for each child.

- Trace shapes from the prints on the acetate using a permanent marker. Put only one shape on each piece of acetate. (You may use a number of shapes from each print.)

- Label the shapes on the top of the acetate as "Shape 1," "Shape 2," etc.

- Make a key for yourself to identify which print each of the shapes came from.

- Lay the acetate sheets in designated spots throughout the room. Display the labeled prints.

- Have the children label their papers from 1 with the number of acetate sheets you made. Explain the game.
  "Your job is to try to find the greatest number of matches in 10-20 minutes. You must use the acetate shapes to find which print the shape comes from. You may have to turn the shape around to find it, but you should keep the side of the acetate with the words 'Shape 1, 2, or 3' toward you. When you find the print where your shape belongs, write the letter on the print next to the number of the shape on your page. For instance, if Shape 4 is found in print D, write D next to number 4 on your paper. Be sure to return the acetate shape to the designated spot when you have finished with it. The person with the greatest number of correct answers at the end of the game wins."

(VARIATIONS MAY INCLUDE LINE FIND, COLOR FIND, PATTERN FIND, ETC.)

SCANNING...

a classroom activity matching written statements with works of art.

- Give each child a different small reproduction.

- Have him/her list ten things that finish this statement: "My painting has...."

- Collect the written statements and the reproductions.

- Mix up both stacks. Tack the reproductions up on the wall.

- Pass out the written papers, making sure no one gets his own paper.

- Let the students try to match the written statements with the reproductions.

- Check each print and description to see if they match. Discuss any discrepancies.

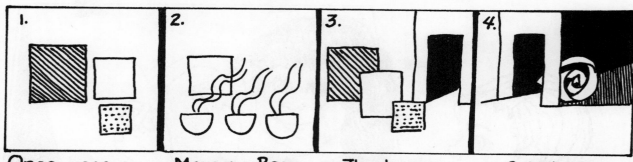

1.	2.	3.	4.
Once upon a time there were three bears.	Mommy Bear fixed breakfast but it was too hot.	The bears went out for a walk.	Goldilocks came in.

It's Goldilocks.

ABSTRACT STORIES...
a creative experience for the class

- On poster board, prepare three abstract stories using familiar children's stories, such as "The Three Bears," "Red Riding Hood," or "The Three Little Pigs."
- Show the abstractions to the class. Tell them what you have done, and see if they can guess what story you have abstracted. Go through each story and point out your abstract symbols.
- Divide the class into smaller groups. Give the groups a prepared list of familiar stories. Let them choose one to illustrate abstractly.
- Share the finished stories.
- Follow-Up: Transfer this technique to an abstract painting. Have the children make up a story based on the abstractions they perceive.

29

DRAWING CHARADES...

a nonverbal vocabulary builder in game format

- Divide the students into groups.
- Supply each group with an easel, paper, and a crayon.
- Explain the game: Each group must try to decode a "Secret Message" by guessing clues given to them on paper by a member of their group. The person in their group who is drawing is "it" and must not talk or write words to give clues. All the groups will be trying to decode the same message at the same time. The first group to guess correctly wins.
- Appoint one child from each group to be "it." Give each of these children the "Secret Message." Signal the groups to start.

Sample "Secret Messages";
  — It is the teacher's birthday.
  — The school is on fire.
  — My dog is lost.
  — Mommy loves daddy.
  — The baby needs a bottle.

- The game can go on for many rounds; each time the group will guess clues from a new "it."

CHAPTER 3

1,000 WORDS WORTH*

*Learning to use words to describe
what we see, feel, and experience
when we look at art.

FEELIE-SOCKS...
learning to describe tactile sensations

Before you begin:
1. Slip plastic cylindrical containers into long tube socks.
2. Label each sock with a letter.
3. Place an object, with a specific characteristic, into each container.

Activities:
*   Have the child reach into the Feelie-socks and describe how the objects feel.
*   Have the child match and describe Feelie-socks that feel the same.
*   Have the child match and describe objects in the Feelie-socks with photographs or magazine illustrations of the same objects.
*   Have the child match and describe an object in the Feelie-sock with pictures of sculpture that have:
    —   similar surface textures
    —   the same basic forms
    —   that are made of the same materials

BOARD SORTING...
manipulating objects while learning vocabulary

• Divide a rectangular poster board into sections. Label the sections:

— circles/squares/triangles/rectangles, etc.
— straight-edged shapes/curved shapes
— open shapes/closed shapes
— geometric shapes/free shapes

• Cut a series of shapes that fit the categories.

• Have the child sort the shapes into the proper sections of the poster board.

(You can adapt Board Sorting to other subjects, such as color sorting, sorting lines, sorting textures, etc.)

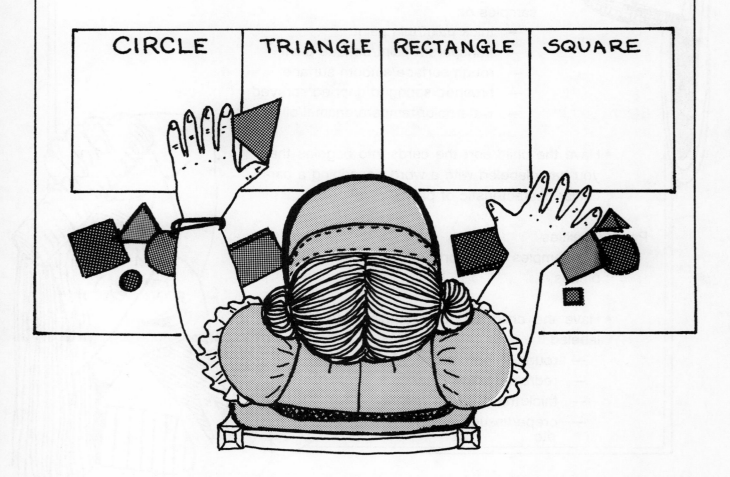

QUALITIES OF MEDIA..

sorting activities designed to teach vocabulary of art
words about media

Paint Qualities

- Prepare 3" x 5" cards with painted surfaces. Include samples of:
  — thick paint/thin paint
  — transparent paint/opaque paint
  — rough surface/smooth surface
  — brushed/sponged/dripped/sprayed
  — watercolor/tempera/enamel/oil

- Have the child sort the cards into baggies that you have labeled with a word describing a particular characteristic of paint.

Paper Qualities

- Cut samples of all sorts of papers into 3" x 5" pieces.

- Have the child sort the samples into baggies labeled:
  — rough/smooth/soft/hard, etc.
  — red/blue/yellow, etc.
  — thick/thin/medium weight
  — crepe/tissue/tracing/toweling, etc.

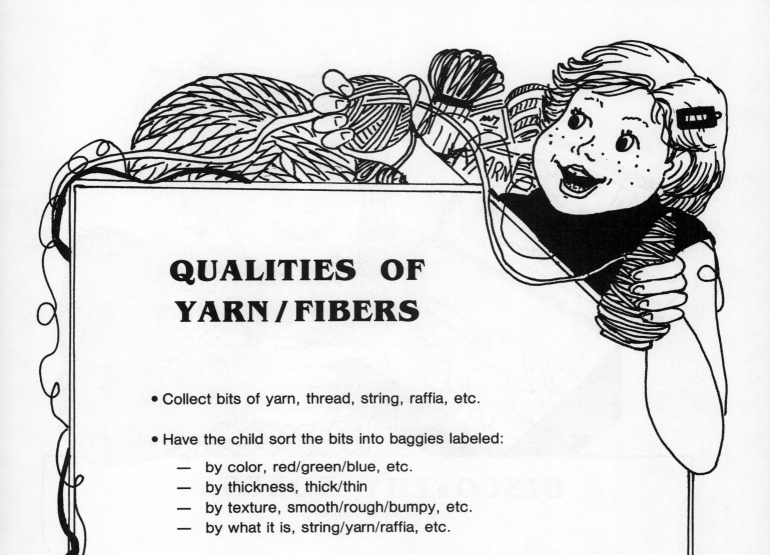

QUALITIES OF YARN / FIBERS

- Collect bits of yarn, thread, string, raffia, etc.

- Have the child sort the bits into baggies labeled:

    — by color, red/green/blue, etc.
    — by thickness, thick/thin
    — by texture, smooth/rough/bumpy, etc.
    — by what it is, string/yarn/raffia, etc.

OTHER MATERIALS

- Have the students examine any media they use and describe the qualities of it. Discuss:

    — color
    — texture
    — shape
    — uses
    — what it is made of
    — how it can be changed

DISCOVERY BOXES...
using art vocabulary

- Collect cardboard (school/cigar) boxes.
- Tape an acetate envelope to the lid.
- Slip a task card* into the envelope.
- Fill the box with appropriate examples.
- Have the student use the discovery box to complete the task.

*Task card examples:

All but one of these items is a photograph. Which one is not a photograph?

All but one of these examples is three dimensional. Which one is not three dimensional?

All but one is made of wood. Which one is not made of wood?

All but one is manmade. Which one is not manmade?

All but one is a clay tool. Which one is not a clay tool?

(Examples in the Discovery Boxes can be labeled with letters of the alphabet and a key provided on the back of each task card for the student to self-check.)

BAG SORTING...

learning vocabulary by sorting

Textures

- Collect and mount photographs, or magazine illustrations, that illustrate one type of texture.

- Have the child sort these examples into baggies labeled:
    — rough/smooth
    — soft/hard
    — shiny/dull

(You may prefer to use actual found objects for the children to sort.)

Crayons

- Collect bits of old broken crayons. Peel the paper off.

- Have the child sort them into baggies labeled:
    — light colors/dark colors
    — warm colors/cool colors
    — red/yellow/blue/green, etc.
    — bright colors/dull colors

FILING PATTERNS...
a learning center activity to expand vocabulary.

- Glue wallpaper samples to 6" x 9" pieces of cardboard.

- Glue identical cardboard boxes together so that the open ends face the front.

- Label the openings with styles of patterns, such as stripes, plaids, dots, checks, prints, and plain; or label the openings with types of repeat, such as regular, irregular, circular, etc.

- Have the child sort the patterns into the categories.

(You can adapt the filing activity to other concepts, such as sorting prints by subject matter, sorting colors, sorting prints by style, etc.)

LANDSCAPE POETRY...
a writing activity using descriptive words

• Choose a variety of landscapes.

• Have each child pick one.

• Tell the children to write:
— one word that describes it
— one short action phrase about it
— one phrase that fits the pattern "as ---as---"
— one other descriptive phrase

• Have the children share their landscape poetry.

(This also works well using their own art-work. It makes a super display when you hang their artwork and their poems.)

POCKET BOARD...
learning the vocabulary of processes.

- On 3" x 5" cards glue photographs, or actual samples, of work made by one specific process.

- Attach tagboard pockets to a poster board to hold the cards.

- Label the pockets:
  - painted
  - printed
  - crayoned
  - woven
  - coiled
  - batiked
  - drawn
  - photographed
  - cut and pasted
  - sewn
  - hammered
  - dyed

- Have the students sort the cards into the proper pockets.

How is it made?
Find the right pocket.

Woven   Drawn   Printed

Painted   Ham

Sewn   Coil   ed

TIME OF DAY...
a classroom discussion

- Choose a series of prints that show specific times of day.
- Have the children group them in categories of:
  - — morning
  - — evening
  - — noon
  - — night
- Discuss the aspects each smaller group of prints has in common. Do they have the same or different amounts of:
  - — activity
  - — shadows
  - — brightness/dullness
  - — subject clues

Related Studio Activity: Have the students draw, or paint pictures that repeat the same settings in morning, noon, and night. Encourage them to use variations of activity, color, shadow, and subject clues to distinguish the chosen time of day. Subjects you might want to suggest include:
- — in the kitchen
- — my house
- — my schoolroom
- — the restaurant

SHAPING FORMS...
a manipulation exercise

- Demonstrate how to shape the following forms out of modeling clay:
  - — a cylinder
  - — a sphere
  - — a cube
  - — a cone
- Have the children make at least one of each of the forms from clay.
- Discuss: "What things can you name that are cylinders, spheres, cubes, or cones?"
- Look at pictures, or slides, of sculptures that are made of combinations of simple forms.
- Have the children name what forms the artist has used.

Related Studio Activity: Have the students combine forms to make their own original sculptures.

IDENTIFY THE FORM...
an activity using tactile clues

- Locate a variety of small forms. You may use wooden building forms, models of geometric solids, or sturdy containers.
- Put one form into each Feelie-sock (p. 32).
- Have the children reach into the Feelie-sock and describe the form inside.
- Prepare a series of cards that show objects that have predominate forms, such as a cylinder, cone, sphere, or cube. You may use any or all of these on the card:
  - — magazine illustrations of common objects
  - — photographs of natural objects
  - — pictures of buildings that have a single form
  - — pictures of sculptures that have a predominate form
- Have the children choose from the stack of cards an object that uses the same form as the one in the Feelie-sock.
- Discuss photographs, slides, or sculptures that use a combination of forms. Have the students locate and describe what forms were used.

CLOSE UP/FAR AWAY...

discussing perspective

- Choose a series of prints that show depth by use of perspective, overlapping, color, and size.

- Discuss ways artists show that some things in their paintings are close to us and some things are far away. Focus on:
  - size...things that are closer appear larger, things far away appear smaller
  - color...things that are closer are usually brighter, things far away duller and lighter
  - overlapping...things closer overlap things behind that are further away
  - perspective...shapes sometimes change to show depth; illustrate on the board by drawing converging railroad tracks, etc.

- Have the children point out where the artists used these ways of showing depth in the examples you chose.

GETTING TO KNOW YOU...

a creative activity interpreting mood

- Choose a large selection of portraits. Let each child choose one he likes best.

- Tell the child to study his portrait choice and try to decide what kind of person the portrait is showing.

- Pair the students and have them introduce their portraits to each other. Have them ask each other questions about their portraits.

- Ask the pairs to pretend they are the people in the portraits and make believe a conversation. Have them demonstrate their conversation for the class.

- Ask the children to explain why they decided certain things about their portrait persons.

- Discuss: Why do artists paint portraits differently?

HOW ARE THEY ALIKE, HOW ARE THEY DIFFERENT?...

a class discussion

- Choose two prints that have many facets in common, but have one main difference.
- Have the children discuss: "How are they alike? How are they different?"

You might choose:

— two prints with similar colors, styles, moods, and time periods but with different subjects

— two prints with similar subjects, styles, time periods, and moods but with different colors

— two prints with similar subjects, styles, moods, and colors, but with different time periods

— two prints with similar colors, styles, time periods, and subjects but with different moods

Of course, you may wish to reverse the whole process and discuss two prints with many differences and only one similarity.

WHICH OF THESE PRINTS BELONG TOGETHER?...

a classroom activity

• Choose six prints, three of which have an element in common, such as
— warm colors/cool colors
— subject
— style
— emotion/mood
— use of line, color, etc.

• Label each print with a letter of the alphabet for easy identification.

• Explain to the class that three of the prints belong together, three do not belong. Ask them to choose which three belong together and tell why.

(Don't panic if your students discover different similarities than you had planned for. Encourage them to find the similarity you had in mind.)

OVERLAPPING...
a class discussion

- Discuss how we can tell that one thing is in front of another when an artist overlaps shapes and objects. Draw examples on the chalkboard or use flannel board shapes.
- Choose a series of prints that have clear examples of overlapping.
- Ask the children to find examples of overlapping in the prints. Have them tell you what is in front.

Related Studio Activity: Have the students draw a crowd scene. Have them put some people in front and some in the back. Challenge them to make a huge crowd. Talk about where you might see a crowd of people - fans at a music concert, the spectators at a game, an army on parade, etc.

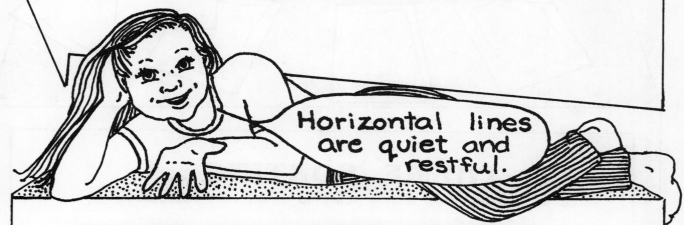

Horizontal lines are quiet and restful.

QUIET OR NOISY MOODS...
interpreting moods

- Choose two paintings that show opposite moods.
- Let the students decide what mood each of them portrays.
- Ask them to decide whether the paintings are noisy and active or quiet and still.
- Discuss: "What has the artist done to make this a (quiet, noisy) painting?"
- Call attention to the differences in the paintings, such as
    — color
    — subject matter
    — use of elements of line, shape, light/dark, etc.
    — style
    — symbols

Suggested Studio Activity: Have each student create a collage that shows the two sides of his/her character — quiet/noisy, cheerful/sad, pleasant/disagreeable. Have students divide their papers in half and choose elements that will illustrate the mood for each side. Remind them to consider color, line, light/dark, and overall arrangement as mood indicators.

THEME SORTING...

a learning center activity designed to help build vocabulary

- Give each child a collection of several small prints.

- Tell the child to sort the small prints into theme categories. Theme categories may include:
  — landscapes
  — still lifes
  — seascapes
  — city scapes
  — portraits
  — animals
  — real events
  — imaginary events

- Look over each child's choices and ask him to explain any choices you disagree with or would have chosen to put in a different category.

CENTER OF INTEREST...

a class discussion

- Choose several prints with distinct centers of interest. Vary your choices by choosing ones that are defined by:
  - — size
  - — position
  - — difference in light and dark areas
  - — color emphasis
  - — shape or line emphasis

- Ask the class to decide what is the center of interest in each of the prints. Have them tell you what the artist has done to make the center of interest stand out.

Related Studio Activity: Have the students paint pictures with distinct centers of interest. Remind them how an artist makes one part of his/her painting more important by selecting a center of interest. Evaluate the paintings for use of a center-of-interest device.

←THIS reminds me of this → Can you tell why?

BODY POSITIONS...
a machine for the learning center

- Cut a 6" tagboard circle and attach it to one end of a 6" x 18" piece of poster board with a paper brad.

- Attach a clear acetate pocket, about 6" x 6", to the end of the poster board opposite the tagboard circle.

- Locate the proper place near the edge of the poster board for a tiny window that will overlap the tagboard circle. Cut it out.

- Locate examples or create cards to slip into the acetate pocket that are:
  - paper shapes
  - emotion words
  - color samples
  - sculpture prints
  - trees
  - furniture
  - architecture
  - animals

- Find examples of people exercising in magazines. Match the body positions to your cards. Glue the pictures of people to the rotating tagboard circle so that they will show through the window as the circle turns.

- Letter on the poster: "This reminds me of this." and "Can you tell why?"

You may want to follow up a session of using this machine at the learning center with writing down, acting out, or discussing slides or pictures of sculptural works in class.

MATCHING TITLES...
two versions

Version A

- Letter several titles or word phrases on cards that may describe a particular print. Include on one of the cards the actual title of the print.

- Pass out the cards to the class. Have each student read his card and tell how it "fits" the print.

- Let the class vote on the title they feel best fits the print.

- Follow up with the facts about the painting and the artist's selected title.

(A variation is to let the students make up their own titles, or phrases, and then proceed as outlined.)

Version B

- Letter a single title on a poster board.

- Mount two or more prints on the board.

- Have the child discuss and choose which print best fits the title.

- Follow up with the facts.

(A variation is to have the student illustrate his idea of what the title would represent first, and then look at the actual print with that title.)

54

DISCUSSING EMOTIONAL EXPRESSIONS

• Choose a series of reproductions that show a variety of emotional expressions.

• Have the children point out:
  — Which one is sad?
  — Which one is mad?
  — Which one is frightened?
  — Which one is bored?

• Discuss what the artist has done, other than change the facial expression, to show how the person is feeling. Could you cover the face and still get the same idea? Consider:
  — body position
  — color
  — situation
  — setting

Variation: Cover the faces of the people in the prints before the children discuss them.

WHERE IS THE LIGHT COMING FROM?...

a class discussion

- Choose a series of prints that have a strong sense of light and dark. They usually have prominent cast shadows.
- Let the students tell you where the light is coming from in each example. Have them explain their decisions. Remind them to consider:
  — the light and dark sides of the objects
  — the shadows
  — where the highlights are

Related Studio Activities:

Have the students draw from observation a collection of geometric forms that are lit by a strong light source. Let them experiment with shading the shapes on their papers.

Have the students draw from imagination one of the following subjects:
— I am walking at night with a flashlight
— Me and my shadow on the playground
— I am in my bedroom at night with the moon shining in the window
— Playing under the streetlight

THE HORIZON LINE...

a class discussion

- Choose a series of prints that shows a variation of placement of the horizon line.

- Discuss the term "horizon line."

- Have the children point out the horizon line in each example.

- Ask: "Why do you think the artist decided to make the horizon line so (high, low, close to the middle) in this painting?"

- Ask: "What if the artist had changed the horizon line from (high, low, or in the middle) to another place? Would it change the picture? How?"

- Ask: "If you were the artist who painted this, would you make the horizon line in the same place or would you change it?"

- Discuss where the horizon line might be in these imaginary examples:
  — We are climbing Mt. Snow
  — The stormy sea
  — The fireworks on the Fourth of July

CHAPTER 4

THE VERDICT*

*Learning to judge and evaluate
works of art based on knowledge.

JUDGEMENTS

Before a child is ready to make a knowledgeable judgement and an honest evaluation about a work of art he must:

A. Be sure to SEE a work of art (Chapter 2).

B. Be able to TALK about a work of art (Chapter 3).

C. Be KNOWLEDGEABLE about the facts he can understand about a work of art.

Knowing the facts about art includes knowing:

1. WHO...facts about the artist
2. WHAT...facts about the work itself
3. WHEN...facts about the time it was made
4. WHERE...facts about the geographic and cultural influences
5. WHY...facts about the reason the work was made
6. HOW...facts about the process by which a work was created

The WHO Facts

Facts about an artist, biographical information, are more important to a child when they give the child insight into:

The Creative Factor...Why did an artist choose to make things his/her own special way? What things did he/she learn from others? What things were his/her own ideas?

A Commitment to Art...What sort of personal decisions, obstacles, or sacrifices did the artist make to pursue his/her career choice? Was it easy for him/her to become an artist, or difficult? Did people of his/her own time like his/her work, or not?

The Relation of Events, Places, People, or Ideas in the Artist's Life to His/Her Work...Are there themes, recurring images, or ideas in the artist's work that we can relate to his/her life?

Ways to Present the WHO Facts:

- Have the class play "To Tell the Truth." The teacher is the host. The class is the panel. Three select members of the class are guests. One of the guests has the facts and will answer the questions truthfully, the other guests will make up answers. The host reads a brief description about the artist's life and the panel asks questions of the three guests. At the end of the questioning period, the panel will vote to decide who is representing the artist and is telling the truth. (A sample list of questions can be given to the panel and guests before play begins and the truthful guest can be given the correct answers.)

- Use films, filmstrips, or books about the artist's life.

- A visitor can impersonate the artist and tell the class about his life.

- Visit an artist, or have an artist visit the class and tell about his life and his work.

- Children can report on particular artists and present their reports to the class dressed in their parts and displaying some of their "works."

- The teacher can give the information verbally or written to the class and follow up with activity pages, such as matching statements, true/false, crossword puzzles, or fill-in-the-blanks.

When we were just in second grade, we could tell a sculpture from a painting!

The WHAT Facts

Other facts about a work of art include WHAT a work of art is. Three facets of this knowledge are:

The Medium...Is it:
    a photograph? (tintype, black and white, color)
    a painting? (oil, watercolor, tempera, acrylic)
    a print? (woodcut, etching, lithograph)
    a sculpture? (free-standing, relief, mobile)
    a weaving?
    a collage?
    a drawing?

The Theme, or Subject...Is it:
    a real event?
    an imaginary event?
    a portrait?
    a still life?
    a landscape?
    an idea?

The Scale...Is it:
    small enough to hold in your hand?
    as big as a grocery bag?
    as big as the teacher's desk?
    as big as the wall in the room?
    as big as the chalkboard?
    bigger than the side of the school?

The WHEN Facts

Sometimes it is important for a child to know WHEN a work of art was made. Dates are usually meaningless to a child unless he can identify a period of time with facts he already knows. Three ways to help a child relate to periods of time are:

Using Visual Clues...

Can you tell by looking if this is a modern painting, or a painting from long ago? How?

What things about this make us think it is a painting from long ago or modern times? Is it:
- the objects in the painting?
- the way people dress?
- the condition of the work? (Is it chipped, cracked?)
- the changes in methods of transportation shown?
- the style?

long ago for sure

Using Personal Time...

This work was made when you were just a baby.

This work was made when your (mother, grandfather, great-grandfather) was your age.

Using Historical Time*...

This was made at the time in history that the television show, *(Little House on the Prairie, The Waltons, M.A.S.H.)* was set.

This was made about the time when (George Washington, Abe Lincoln, John Kennedy) was President of our country.

This was made about the time Christopher Columbus sailed.

This was made in the time of knights and castles.

This was made in the time of Jesus.

*Do not discuss historical time unless the children have some concept of history. Historical time has most meaning for children in grades 4-6.

Asia...
all right!

The WHERE Facts

Closely related to WHEN a work was made is WHERE it was made. Facts concerning the location may be seen in the work itself. Consider:

Are there any characteristics of the work that are typical of a geographic location or that show a cultural influence?

Did the place where this was made have any influence on:
   the process or technique used?
   the selection of materials?
   the theme or subjects?
   regional or cultural symbols?
   style?
   function?
   scale?

The HOW Facts

Children understand HOW best when they themselves have actually done work by the process. Methods they have observed are also familiar. However, more elaborate processes, basic ones done on a large scale, or ones done with unfamiliar materials, should be explained or demonstrated so the children can have a clear understanding of HOW a work of art was made. Actual samples of raw materials, or tools, can be passed around for the children to examine. When possible the children should participate in the process themselves to get a more accurate knowledge of how a work of art was made.

The WHY Facts

Some works of art are best understood if the children learn WHY it was made. The reasons artists have made things are as diverse as people themselves; however, this list might prove helpful:

There is:

Art with magical powers
Art that tells a religious message or story
Art that records an historical event
Art that records a way of feeling
Art as decoration
Art as a monument
Art as a protest
Art that visualizes our fantasies

so that's why!

...the list is endless, but a key question is:

"WHY DO YOU THINK THE ARTIST MADE THIS?"

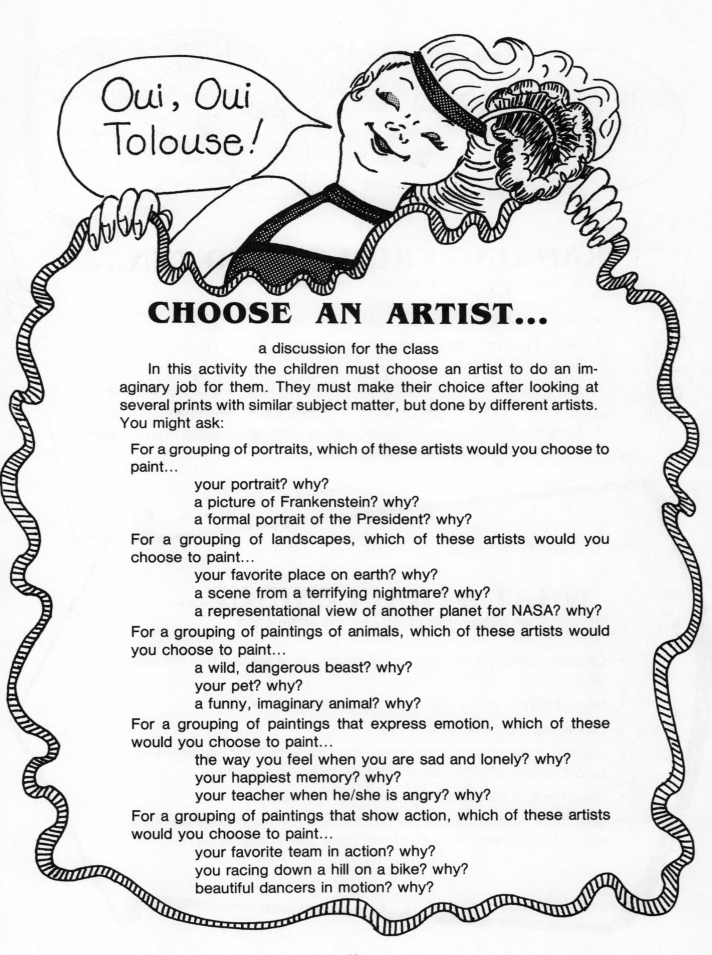

Oui, Oui Tolouse!

CHOOSE AN ARTIST...

a discussion for the class

In this activity the children must choose an artist to do an imaginary job for them. They must make their choice after looking at several prints with similar subject matter, but done by different artists. You might ask:

For a grouping of portraits, which of these artists would you choose to paint...

        your portrait? why?

        a picture of Frankenstein? why?

        a formal portrait of the President? why?

For a grouping of landscapes, which of these artists would you choose to paint...

        your favorite place on earth? why?

        a scene from a terrifying nightmare? why?

        a representational view of another planet for NASA? why?

For a grouping of paintings of animals, which of these artists would you choose to paint...

        a wild, dangerous beast? why?

        your pet? why?

        a funny, imaginary animal? why?

For a grouping of paintings that express emotion, which of these would you choose to paint...

        the way you feel when you are sad and lonely? why?

        your happiest memory? why?

        your teacher when he/she is angry? why?

For a grouping of paintings that show action, which of these artists would you choose to paint...

        your favorite team in action? why?

        you racing down a hill on a bike? why?

        beautiful dancers in motion? why?

RANKING FROM ONE TO TEN...
a learning center activity

- Give two children the same set of ten prints.

- Have them rank their print set in order from 1 (least liked) to 10 (best liked).

- Have each child briefly explain why he/she made his or her decisions. Why was a certain print ranked fifth and the next one sixth?

- Have the children compare their ranking order and explain to each other why they made their particular choices.

WHAT'S HAPPENING?...
an interpreting activity for the entire class

- Choose a print with storytelling value, groups of people, or a dramatic situation.

- Show the print to the class but do not discuss the print.

- Divide the class into groups.

- Have them act out, or write down, their ideas of what happened just before or just after the artist stopped time in the painting.

- Have the groups share their ideas with the class.

- Give them the facts about the painting and ask them to decide if the artist chose to stop the action at a good time in his/her work.

Contemporary Printmaking

A guide to the techniques and care of prints in
conjunction with an exhibition of 50 prints from
the permanent collection of Ashland Oil, Inc.

Ashland Oil, Inc., began a collection of works of
art several years ago. It did so partly with the
thought of decorating its offices attractively, but
the company also sought to make the working
places of its employees more stimulating and
conducive to creative effort.

Recently Ashland selected 50 prints from the
more than 600 now in its collection and is making
them available for public exhibition.

This folder describes techniques used in printmaking, offers guidance in caring for them properly, and defines some of the terms associated
with printmaking. As such, it is a brief in-
troduction to a subject now rapidly gaining in interest among both artists and the viewers of their
works.

The Relief Print

The oldest method of printmaking is the relief
print, which includes the woodcut, wood engraving and linoleum print (or lino cut). A wood or linoleum block is worked on directly by the artist,
who cuts out areas which are not to be printed.
The surface of the block, which stands in relief, is
inked and the block is printed on paper by use of
a press or by burnishing the paper with a rubbing
motion.

The woodcut is produced from a block cut in
the direction of the grain to yield a relief image
which prints black lines. In wood engraving, however, the image is conceived as white lines (which
are cut away) on a black ground (which is left in
relief). The image is cut on a block of end-grain
wood on which the grain of the wood runs at a
right angle to the surface of the block. The woodcut is done with a knife and gouge and the wood
engraving is done with finer engraving tools.
These concepts are not confining, however, as
some artists may produce an image in black lines
on an end-grain block.

The approach to making a linoleum cut, or lino
cut, is similar to that for a woodcut. Linoleum,
however, is flexible and has no grain, so the artist
can cut freely in any direction.

The printing of a relief block is as important as
the cutting. Thin Japanese paper is placed over
the inked block, which is then rubbed with a
spoon or similar instrument from the center out-
ward. Hand printing gives the artist more control
over the medium. For large editions, or when the
block is incorporated with type, the relief block
may be printed with a press which usually works
in a single downward pressing motion.

The Intaglio Print

The intaglio process (Italian, from *intagliare,* to
engrave) is one in which the artist scores an image into a metal surface by hand with a pointed
tool or by the use of acids. The three basic intaglio processes are engraving, drypoint, and
etching.

Engraving is the oldest of the intaglio processes. The basic tool is a burin or graver which is
pushed across a metal plate. The burin is a hard
steel tool which removes a threadlike curl of metal
as it is moved across the plate. The gouging action raises a ridge of metal, or burr, at the side of
the line; this is removed with a scraper to achieve
the characteristic sharpness of line.

Drypoint differs from engraving in that a sharp
needle is pulled across the plate to scratch a faint
line. The action raises a burr which is retained
and which holds more ink than the line itself. A
drypoint print is characterized by soft, modulated,
velvety lines.

Etching is an intaglio process which utilizes the
action of acid to *bite* a line into the plate. The
plate, generally copper, is covered with an acid
resistant material that protects the plate.

The ground is melted or poured onto the plate

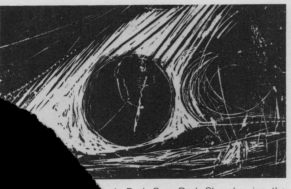

...no's Dark Sea, Dark Sky *showing the
...ses achieved in the woodcut. Notice
...imple roulette tool wheeled across*

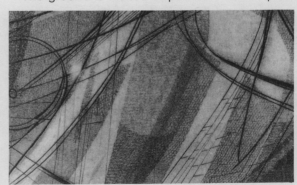

*The various threadlike even lines were achieved with line
etching, while the tonal areas were accomplished by pressing
several different mesh screens in soft ground in Stanley
William Hayter's* Pegase.

*...ie Schuselka's
...ache can also*

and spread to a thin, even coating. Drawing is done with any pointed instrument which scratches the ground away to expose the metal. The plate is then submerged in an acid bath which eats, or etches, the exposed metal.

The finished intaglio plate is inked and placed face up on the bed of a press and uniformly dampened paper is placed on top of it. Blotters and felt blankets are laid over the paper, and these are passed slowly through the two steel rollers of the press under great pressure. The paper, made pliable by dampening, is forced into the depressions of the plate, where it picks up the ink left after wiping.

The Planographic Print

Planography is the process of printing from a smooth surface, as in lithography or offset lithography.

Lithography (from the Greek "lithos," for stone) is a medium which facilitates the development of rich tonal patterns, as attained in crayon drawings. Unlike the relief and intaglio processes that depend on a physical separation of area to be inked, lithography is based on the antipathy of grease and water.

The traditional material used in the process is a block of German limestone at least two inches thick. The surface of the stone is ground flat and smooth, then washed and dried. The stone is very sensitive to grease and must be handled carefully. An image can be created on it with traditional materials such as lithographic crayons and tusche; the newer processes of transfers and rubbings; the use of unorthodox solvents with tusche; and photographic processes. After the stone is printed the surface can be reground and used again. Zinc and aluminum plates are now used frequently, especially in the photo-lithographic processes, as they are cheaper, lighter and store more easily.

After the image is drawn, the surface of the stone is *etched*. Unlike the intaglio process, the lithographic etch does not eat away at the stone

but merely *fixes* the image. The excess crayon and tusche are removed with turpentine in a process called *washing out*. For editions of 50 or more a second etch insures a deeper penetration of the image. The stone is then ready to print.

Water is sponged over the surface of the prepared stone. It is repelled by the greasy drawing, and helps prevent the greasy ink from adhering to the undrawn portions of the stone. Ink is applied with a roller until the image is sufficiently built up. An impression is then taken from the stone, using a lithographic press which works in a sliding and scraping motion.

The Stencil Print

The stencil print is created by passing ink over a stencil, a stiff material which has a desired form cut out to allow ink to pass through and recreate the form on paper.

Serigraphy is the form of stencil printing which uses silk, organdy or a similar open-meshed material to hold the stenciling substance, which may be some form of glue, lacquer, photographic stencil or cut-film stencil. The material, usually silk is stretched over a frame. Areas not to be printed are stopped-out—the holes in the mesh are filled so ink will not pass through.

The tusche-and-glue method works on the same concept as lift-ground etching in intaglio, and it is based on the principle that grease resists water. The image is painted or drawn on the screen with a liquid or crayon form of tusche, a greasy substance. The screen then is covered with a glue compound which is repelled by the tusche and fills the remainder of the screen. The tusche is then washed out with kerosene or turpentine and the screen is ready to print.

The cut-film stencil process, similar to the paper stencil, uses a colored film of lacquer laminated to a paper or plastic backing, available commercially. Areas to be printed are carefully cut with a sharp knife and stripped away. The film is then adhered with heat or a solvent to the underside of the stretched screen and the backing

Robert Kipniss used a lithographic crayon for his untitled landscape. The texture is due in part to the roughness of the stone's surface.

The texture of silk is apparent in the Sky Rooms. *The relationship of its* be seen.

Detail of Clare Romai. bold, solid lines and mas. the results from using a the block.

is peeled away. This process leaves a perfect stencil of lacquer film ready to print and lends itself to precision edged shapes.

When the screen is ready for printing it is placed over the paper, and ink is worked through the open parts by pulling a squeegee, a rubber blade set in a handle, across the screen. After the final printing, the stencil image can be cleaned off and the screen used again for other designs. A great attraction of serigraphy is that only three basic pieces of easily constructed equipment are required: the screen, squeegee and drying rack.

The Care and Collecting of Prints

The care and preservation of a print collection requires much attention, and this section is intended to alert the collector to the dangers of improper handling, mounting, matting, framing and display.

Loose prints should be handled as little as possible, and then only with clean hands. The inked surface is as vulnerable to abuse as the paper itself. Never touch the surface of a print or cause the paper to crease, as this may make the ink crack or damage the fiber of the paper.

Unframed prints should be stored in drawers or cases, separated by sheets of tissue or glassine paper. It is advisable, however, to mount each print as this adds vital protection. Mounting is a process of backing each print with a sturdy support to prevent it from bending or creasing when handled. Further protection is achieved in matting. The mat prevents other objects—such as other prints or glass—from coming in contact with the inked surface. Mats and mounting boards should always be composed of 100 per cent rag which is acid free. The acids in chipboard, corrugated board and cardboard made of wood pulp will stain the print in a relatively short time and often transfer the patterns of their construction, such as corrugations, to the print itself.

Whether purchased loose or framed, prints should *never* be altered by an owner or framer in any way. They should never be trimmed to fit frames, flattened, drymounted or glued, repaired in any way (such as taping, erasing or touching up), nor should old hinges be soaked or torn off. Any such alterations are considered aesthetic violations which may drastically lessen the commercial value of the print.

Prints are attached to the mounting board—never to the mat—with hinges. This allows the mat to be opened and the print examined as it lies flat. Only hinges made from Japanese paper attached with old-fashioned vegetable library paste, or hinges made from gummed linen tape, should be used. Common pressure-sensitive cellophane or masking tapes should never be used as they are acidic and will stain the print in time; they also tend to dry out and lose their adhering qualities. They are often used on the incorrect assumption that what doesn't show will not hurt.

The hinges should be weaker than the paper of the art work itself so that under stress the hinge will give way rather than the print. At least two hinges for small works, and more for larger works, should be fastened to the top back of the print. This lets the print hang freely as well as to breathe—that is, to shrink and expand with changes in humidity.

Framing is a means of offering a print the protection it needs while on permanent display. A work should never be exposed for any length of time without a glass covering. The print should never come in contact with the glass as it may adhere to the glass surface and be damaged when removed. Contact also increases the danger of condensation on the print surface. Matting will help prevent condensation. In the case of unmatted prints, fillets—narrow strips of material in the framing—will keep the print and glass from contact. Glass is the preferred covering but plexiglas can be used, although it scratches easily and attracts dust. Non-glare glass should be avoided for aesthetic reasons, as it greatly distorts the tonal qualities of the work. Finally, the frames should be sealed to eliminate the penetration of dust.

When a print has been properly mounted, matted and framed, it is still a vulnerable work of art. Temperature, humidity and lighting all affect works on paper. The best lighting is a subdued incandescent light. Direct sunlight, strong indirect sunlight and fluorescent lighting should be avoided, especailly with color prints. Strong lighting has a deteriorating effect, causing colors to fade and paper to discolor and become brittle. If possible, it is wise to rotate one's collection, viewing works at intervals and otherwise keeping them stored. Humidity is another important factor, as microbiological organisms will thrive if exposed to a relative humidity of 75 per cent for a short time. The ideal humidity is between 50 per cent and 60 per cent. A steady humidity and temperature help prevent rippling. Works should never be displayed in rooms or areas which are apt to have constantly high, low, or variable humidity and temperature readings, such as kitchens, bathrooms, near outside doors, or over fireplaces or other heating and cooling units.

A print damaged in any way will require the care of a professional conservator. The best safeguard against unscrupulous "restoration" is a little knowledge of the field on the part of the collector. It bears repeating that tears should never be repaired, margins should never be trimmed, and no changes should ever be attempted by anyone other than an expert paper conservator.

Glossary

artist's proof: Any impression printed especially for or retained by the artist for the artist's own use, usually so marked (A.P. or artist's proof) and not normally numbered. When numbered, the system will be different from the regular edition; such as Arabic numerals for the edition and Roman numerals for the artist's proofs.

bon à tirer: The notation (French, "good to pull") indicating the approval of a proof by the artist as the standard of quality for the edition. Also indicated by "printer's proof," or "BAT."

cancellation proof: When an edition has been completed the artist *cancels* or *effaces* his plate, stone, block or screen by defacing the image, usually with an "X" across the surface. Occasionally an intaglio plate will be *punched,* that is, holes will be made in each corner. An impression is then pulled to prove the limiting of the edition. (These are not to be confused with prints pulled from cancelled plates without the artist's approval and usually after his death.)

chop (chopmark, seal): A printed or stamped symbol used by printers, workshops, artists and collectors as an identification which may be inked or embossed (blindstamp, drystamp).

edition: The total prints of a single image numbered and signed by the artist. The size of an edition is indicated by the denominator of the fraction located at the bottom margin of the impression. The size of the edition may be influenced by the technique used but is more often arbitrary. Artist's proofs, trial proofs, printer's proofs, etc., are not included as part of the edition so the edition number may not be a clear indication of all impressions extant.

impression: An image produced by transferring ink from one surface to another, or by transferring a shape from one surface to another as in embossing.

livre de luxe: A handmade book of original prints and text, usually housed in a slipcase, folder or binding.

numbering: The system by which the total quantity of prints in an edition is indicated by the denominator of a fraction with the individual prints identified by the numerator, traditionally done in pencil at the lower left or center of image. The numerator was once considered an indication of the order in which the prints were pulled. It was thought that the quality of the impression lessened as prints were pulled, but each print should be identical making such interpretations incorrect. Numbering is now considered a record keeping device. Occasionally the inscription will indicate the total only.

presentation proof: An impression (usually carrying a personal inscription) which an artist may present to an individual in a workshop situation.

proof: An impression taken at any stage in the making of a print that is not part of the edition, which may include printer's proofs, experimental proofs, progressive proofs, artist's proofs, cancellation proofs, presentation proofs, trial proofs, or special impressions for the workshop in which an edition is printed.

reproduction: A graphic work normally made through photomechanical techniques of another work of art which the artist intended to be unique. Reproductions are not considered original fine prints. Pre-20th century methods of *copying* unique works in such media as mezzotints for books and wood engravings for books and newspapers are considered original but should be valued primarily for the technical achievements of the engraver and not for the unique work copied.

restrike: A print (beyond the original edition) made from an artist's original plate, stone, block or stencil and usually printed in unlimited numbers after the artist's death. Such prints are usually identified by a worn impression, different quality paper or ink, or obvious alterations. Many worn plates are steel-faced for long runs or reworked in an effort to regain the clarity of the artist's first impressions. (Any "restrike" by an artist from a plate not cancelled should be identified as a *second edition.*)

signature: The custom of signing and numbering prints is less than a hundred years old. It is taken as an approval of the print by the artist. The inclusion of an artist's signature that is part of the medium does not establish this approval. Signatures are usually in pencil in the lower right below the image, but the practice varies widely.

state: A proof (to guide the artist's progress) that shows a print in a particular stage of development.

suite: Prints related in theme or image and sometimes in technique, often issued in a portfolio.

trial proof: An early proof, often incorporating the artist's revisions, pulled during the attempt to stabilize the image technically and aesthetically.

working proof: A trial proof bearing the artist's or printer's notes and corrections.

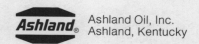

Ashland Oil, Inc.
Ashland, Kentucky

HANG IT...

a class discussion

- Choose a series of prints with a variety of subjects, styles, artists, and colors.

- Have the class discuss the characteristics of each print.

- Ask each child to decide:

   - Which one would you hang in your bedroom? Why?

   - Which one would you hang in the kitchen? Why?

   - Which one would you hang in the living room? Why?

   - If you were the manager of a large hotel, which one would you choose for the lobby? Why?

   - If you were decorating the main hall of a stately old castle, which one would you pick? Why?

      - Discuss the characteristics of each print and talk about why people in the class choose the same or different places to hang it.

SOUNDS LIKE...

matching sounds and prints

Version A for the learning center

- Select a number of small prints and label them with letters of the alphabet.

- Choose the same number of brief musical melodies that match each print. Record the melodies on tape indicating at the start of each a number to identify it.

- Have the child match each melody with a print and record on a piece of paper the number and letter of the matches.

- Have the child tell why he/she chose each print to match the melodies.

Version B for the entire class

- Choose a series of prints for the whole class to view at once.

- Label the prints with letters of the alphabet.

- Choose a recording that fits one of the prints but not the others.

- Play the recording for the class. Have them match the music with the print it fits best.

- Discuss how music and art are related. Have the student share examples of how art and music are used together in modern society.

Related Studio Activity: Have the children make their own slides and set them in sequence with music and sounds.

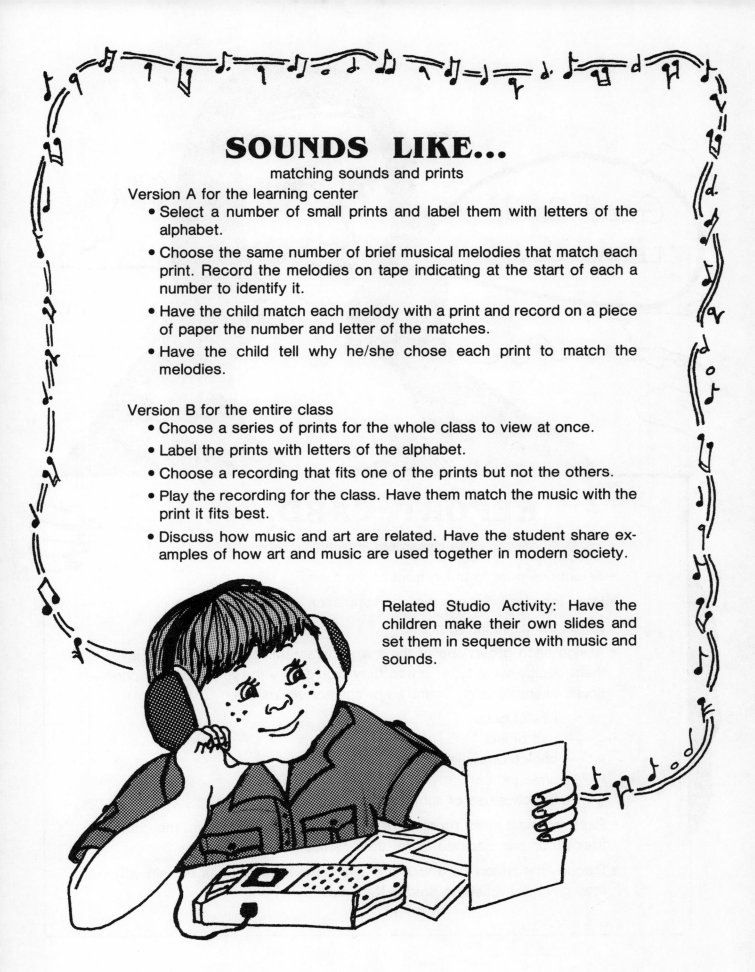

REPORT CARD...

a classroom activity

- Select one print to put in front of the room.

- Have the class discuss the characteristics of the print.

- Divide the class into groups.

- Assign each group one of the main characteristics of the print. Have them decide what letter grade they would give the artist for that particular characteristic. Examples of characteristics are:
  - use of color
  - use of line
  - choice of subject
  - arrangement
  - effective use of light and dark

- Pass around a mock report card and have the groups record the grade their group has decided on for their particular characteristic.

- Discuss the report card with the class. Have the groups explain why they gave the artist the grades they did.

PICKING PORTRAIT PEOPLE...
a class discussion

- Display a series of large prints of portraits. Label each of the prints with a letter of the alphabet.

- Discuss:
  — Who would you pick to be your best friend? Why?
  — Who would you pick to be your parent? Why?
  — Who would you pick to be with to have the most fun? Why?
  — Who would you pick to be a person to stay away from? Why?
  — Who would you pick to star in a war movie? a love story?
  — Who would you choose to be you in another time? Why?
  — Who do you think was the hardest subject for the artist to paint? Why?

WHAT IF...
a class discussion

- Choose a print with strong emotional impact.
- Discuss the ways the artist has shown the mood. How did his/her choices affect the final outcome? Talk about:
  - the colors
  - the types of lines
  - the textures
  - the shapes
  - the arrangement of objects
- Ask: Would it make a difference if he/she had changed:
  - the colors
  - the types of lines
  - the textures
  - the shapes
  - the arrangement of objects

Related Studio Activity: Have the students do the same drawing four ways: once with straight lines, once with curved lines, once with broken lines, and once with curly lines. Discuss the differences in the drawings with the varying lines.

It wouldn't be the same!

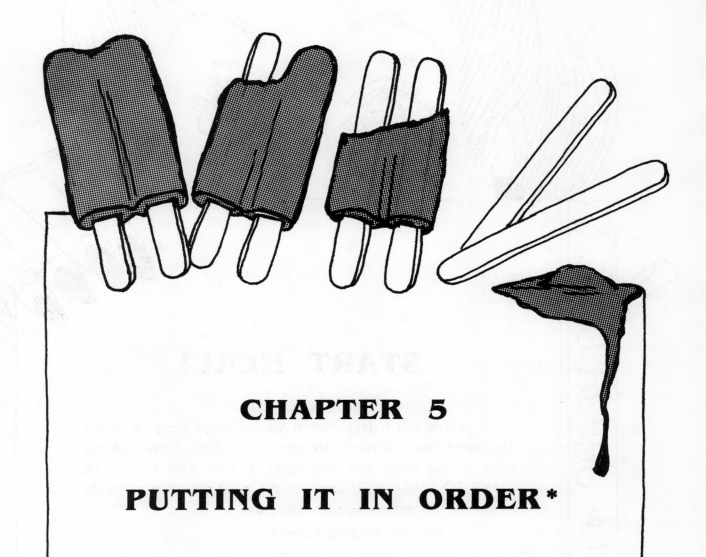

CHAPTER 5

PUTTING IT IN ORDER*

*Sequencing and Organizing
Suggestions

START HERE!

If you're still hiding behind your college copy of *Three Thousand Years of World Art*, step out, put that heavy volume back on the shelf, and take heart. THERE ARE PAINLESS WAYS TO ORGANIZE. Some of the most effective methods (great for elementary age children) are:

- Key into Existing Format
- Use a Studio-Based Plan
- Try a Theme Study

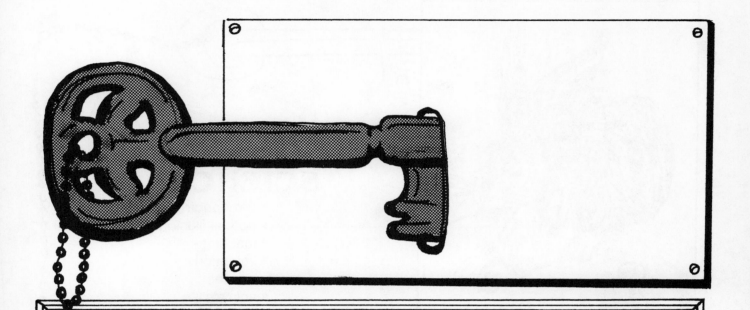

EXISTING FORMAT

Basic education concepts can be reinforced by using art study along with more traditional methods in each subject area. Any subject can be expanded to include relevant artwork. Brainstorm subject areas and search out art examples to fit your needs. Typical examples for each subject area are illustrated on the following pages, along with discussion topics that might serve as springboards. Studio projects that relate to the focus of the lesson can be included. Emphasis should always be open ended, not a copy of the artwork.

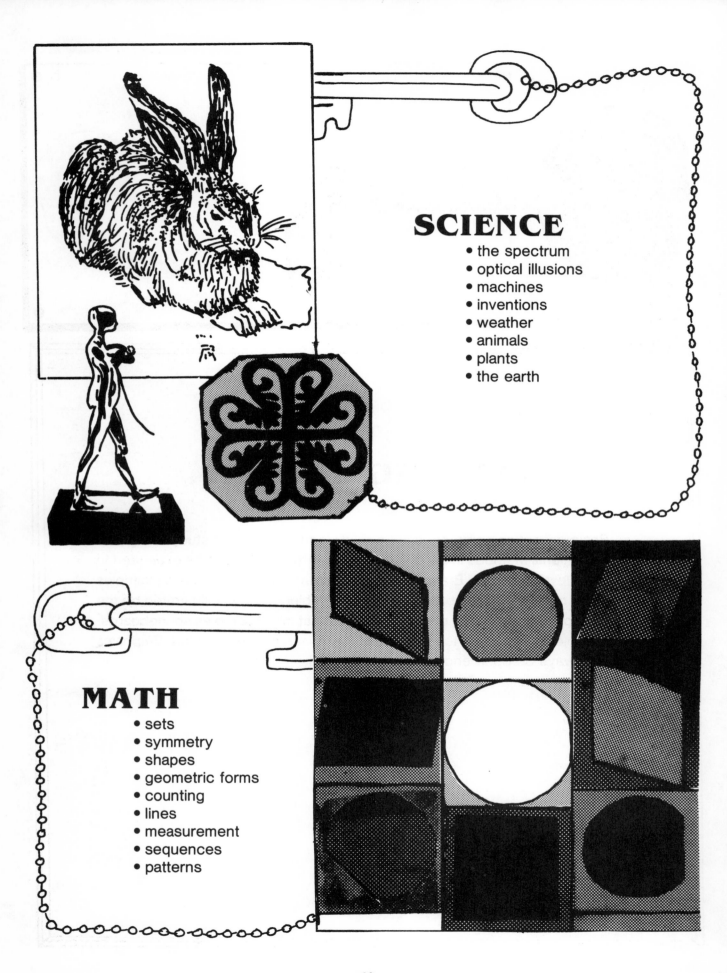

SCIENCE

- the spectrum
- optical illusions
- machines
- inventions
- weather
- animals
- plants
- the earth

MATH

- sets
- symmetry
- shapes
- geometric forms
- counting
- lines
- measurement
- sequences
- patterns

SOCIAL STUDIES

- architecture
- tools
- natural resources
- religion
- costume
- folklore
- customs
- history
- heroes
- transportation
- cities

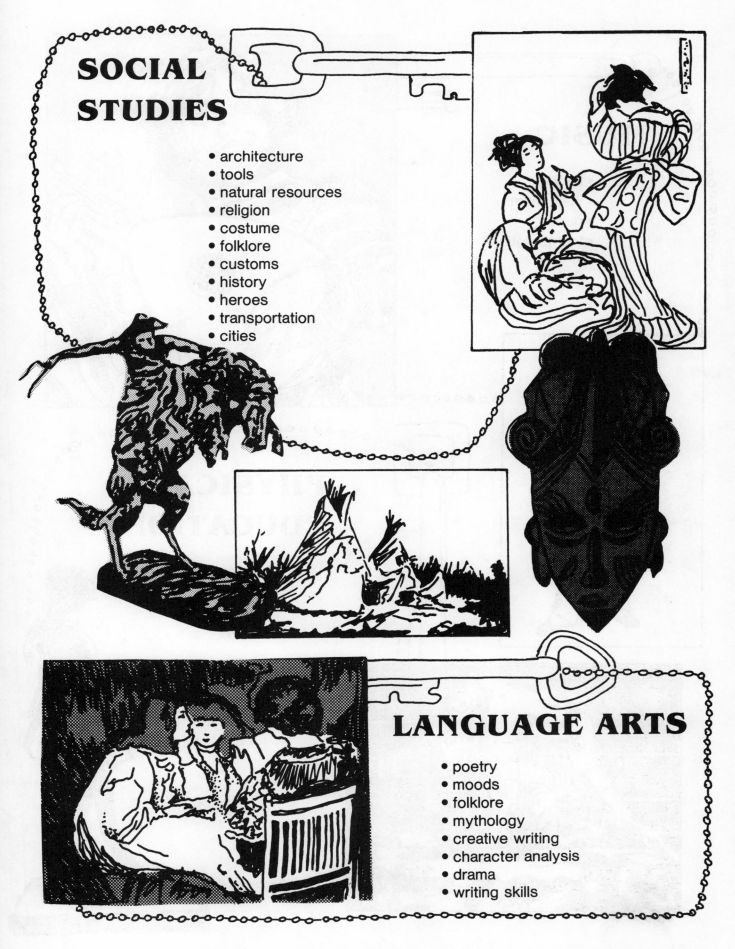

LANGUAGE ARTS

- poetry
- moods
- folklore
- mythology
- creative writing
- character analysis
- drama
- writing skills

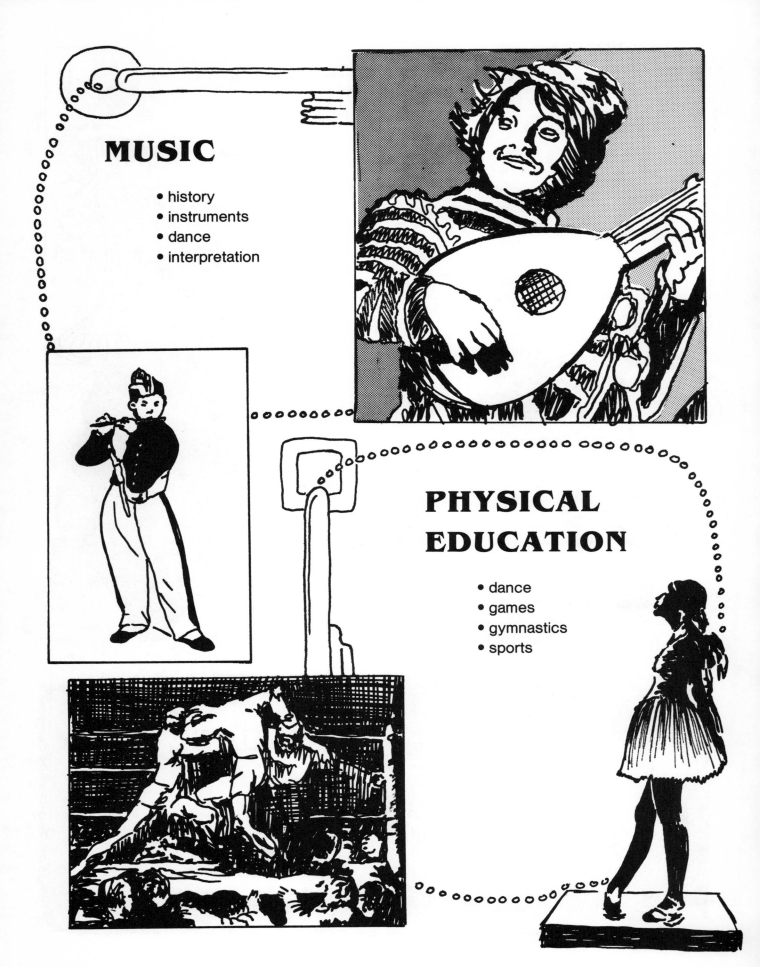

MUSIC

- history
- instruments
- dance
- interpretation

PHYSICAL EDUCATION

- dance
- games
- gymnastics
- sports

STUDIO-BASED

Studio-based programs follow many formats. Some studio programs emphasize the elements of art, some are media based, some concentrate on skills or techniques. Whatever the emphasis, art appreciation included in the program adds to a child's basic understanding of the art studio concepts. Looking, talking, and evaluating can be done before or after a working session. Some teachers set up "Looking Corners" to use during work time for students to refer to. The skills developed through the appreciation sessions serve to motivate and help the child evaluate his own work. Examples of topics included in studio-based programs that will also encompass areas of discussion in art appreciation are: The Elements of Art Skills and Techniques Media

THE ELEMENTS OF ART

- texture
- line
- color
- shape/form
- pattern
- light/dark
- motion
- composition

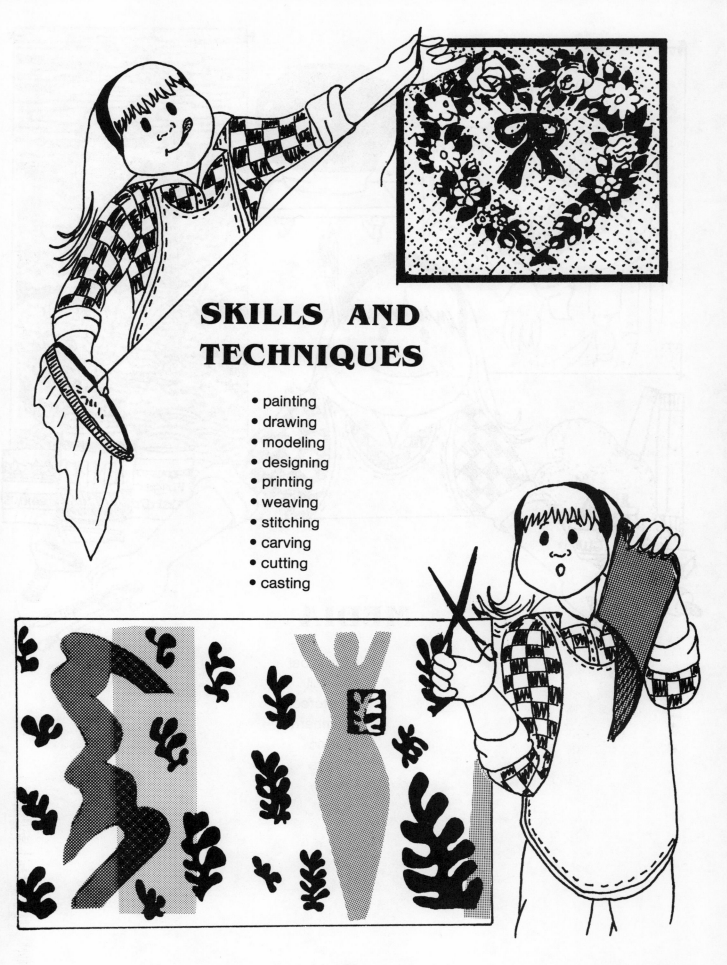

SKILLS AND TECHNIQUES

- painting
- drawing
- modeling
- designing
- printing
- weaving
- stitching
- carving
- cutting
- casting

MEDIA

- charcoal
- pencil
- watercolor
- tempera
- fabric
- fibers
- paper
- clay

THEME STUDY

A theme study organizes artwork by subject or categories. This system works well in a self-contained classroom or an art room setting. Topics for theme study vary from broad categories to specific examples of one subject. Typical examples often used at the elementary level are:

- Still lifes
- Portraits
- Landscapes
- Interiors
- Make-Believe
- Real Events
- Famous People
- Ordinary People
- Animals
    - horses
    - cats
    - dogs
    - farm animals

- Children
- Families
- Mother and Child
- Games
- Cities and Farms
- The Sea
- Transportation
- Dreams
- The Circus
- Sports

A definite advantage of the theme-study format is that the teacher can take advantage of the particular interests of the students in the class.

MOTHER AND CHILD

- media
- arrangement
- mood
- technique
- use of color
- shapes

FLOWERS

- arrangement
- color
- mood
- technique
- media
- style

THE FAVORITE CAT

CATS

- purpose
- media
- technique
- mood
- texture
- symbols

WHO TEACHES?

School situations vary. What works for one district may not work for another. Here are a couple of suggestions that might work for you.

...THE PICTURE LADY

Some schools use parents and community volunteers to teach elementary art appreciation. These volunteers are given prints and related study materials by a staff member. The materials might include a biography of the artist, facts about the painting, sample questions, activities, and related examples. The volunteer prepares a mini-lesson about a particular print and visits the class to present the material. The nice thing about this system is that students get the unspoken message that art is important to many people...not just teachers.

...THE TEAM AND THE TRAVELING SHOW

A group of teachers can get together and make up a traveling art show program. The materials would be passed from room to room. When more than one teacher prepares for the show, it lightens the load. Title cards, informational lettering, photographs, prints, and studio suggestions could be included in a packet that would travel with each print. (What classroom teacher wouldn't love to have several bulletin boards for the initial investment of making just one!) The group efforts add to the quality of materials as improvements, new ideas, and adjustments are made in the packet.